KEATON CAMPBELL

You've Been LIED to: The Revealing Truth Behind Our Financial System and our Governments.

Copyright © 2023 by Keaton Campbell

All rights reserved. No part of this publication may be reproduced, stored or transmitted in any form or by any means, electronic, mechanical, photocopying, recording, scanning, or otherwise without written permission from the publisher. It is illegal to copy this book, post it to a website, or distribute it by any other means without permission.

Keaton Campbell asserts the moral right to be identified as the author of this work.

Keaton Campbell has no responsibility for the persistence or accuracy of URLs for external or third-party Internet Websites referred to in this publication and does not guarantee that any content on such Websites is, or will remain, accurate or appropriate.

First edition

This book was professionally typeset on Reedsy. Find out more at reedsy.com

Contents

Chapter 1: The Pyramid Scheme	1
Chapter 2: The Rise and Fall of Fiat Currencies	3
Chapter 3: Who Owns Our Money?	5
Chapter 4: The Birth of the IRS and its Connection to the...	7
Chapter 5: The Silver Standard of 1933 and the Loss of Real...	9
Chapter 6: The Introduction of Paper Money	12
Chapter 7: Systematic Loopholes	14
Chapter 8: Recap & Wrap up	16
SIDE NOTE-Goes Along With Chapter 4	18

Chapter 1: The Pyramid Scheme

The monetary system is a complex web of relationships that many people are unaware of. At the top of this pyramid scheme is the Federal Reserve, the central bank of the United States. It is responsible for printing and distributing money throughout the country. However, this money is not distributed equally. Instead, it flows to the largest banks and corporations in the country.

The big banks have the power to create money through the fractional reserve banking system. This system allows banks to lend out more money than they actually have in reserves. The result is an increase in the money supply, which can lead to inflation. The banks make money by charging interest on the loans they make, and they use this money to invest in the stock market and other profitable ventures.

The largest corporations in the country have the power to control the banks through their use of credit. They use their wealth and power to influence government policies that benefit their interests, such as tax breaks and deregulation. These corporations often fund political campaigns, and as a result, politicians are beholden to them.

This system creates a vicious cycle where the Federal Reserve prints money, which flows to the big banks and corporations, who then use their power to control government policies. The government, in turn, enforces policies that benefit the wealthy at the expense of the average citizen.

The result of this system is a growing wealth gap between the rich and poor. The top 1% of the population controls an increasingly large share of the wealth, while the middle class and working poor struggle to make ends meet. The system is rigged against the average citizen, and it is time for change.

In conclusion, the monetary system is a pyramid scheme that benefits the wealthy at the expense of the average citizen. The Federal Reserve prints money, which flows to the big banks and corporations, who then use their power to control government policies. This cycle must be broken if we are to create a more equitable society where everyone has a fair chance to succeed.

Chapter 2: The Rise and Fall of Fiat Currencies

Money is an essential part of our daily lives. We use it to buy goods and services, pay bills, and save for the future. But have you ever wondered what gives money its value? In the past, money was typically tied to a physical commodity like gold or silver, but today, most money is considered fiat currency.

Fiat currency is a type of money that is not backed by any physical commodity but is instead backed by the government that issued it. This means that the value of fiat currency is not derived from its intrinsic value, but rather from the trust people have in the government that issued it.

The use of fiat currency is not a new concept; it has been used for centuries. However, history has shown that fiat currencies have a limited lifespan. Throughout history, many currencies have risen to power only to eventually fall out of use. The reasons for this can be diverse, but one thing is certain: all fiat currencies have an expiration date.

In ancient times, rulers and emperors would often issue coins with their image on them to assert their power and authority. These coins were made from precious metals like gold or silver, and their value was derived from the value of the metal itself. However, as civilizations grew more complex and trade expanded, the need for a more flexible form of currency emerged. This led to the creation of paper money.

The first paper money was issued in China during the Tang dynasty in the 7th century. It was a form of fiat currency that was backed by the government's authority. Paper money allowed for greater flexibility in trade and commerce and quickly spread to other parts of the world. By the 20th century, most countries had abandoned the gold standard and had adopted fiat currency.

While fiat currency has many advantages, such as flexibility and ease of use, it also has its drawbacks. The most significant risk is the loss of trust in the government that issued the currency. When people lose faith in their government's ability to manage the economy, they may lose confidence in the currency, causing its value to plummet.

Throughout history, we have seen many examples of this. In the early 1920s, Germany experienced hyperinflation, where the value of their currency became practically worthless. More recently, Venezuela has experienced a similar situation, where hyperinflation has led to widespread poverty and economic instability.

In conclusion, while fiat currency has been a staple of modern economies for centuries, it is not invincible. Throughout history, we have seen many examples of fiat currencies losing their value, and there is no reason to believe that it will not happen again. The key to the longevity of a currency is the trust people have in the government that issued it.

Chapter 3: Who Owns Our Money?

When we think of money, we often assume that the government is the one who owns it and prints it. However, this is not entirely accurate. In the United States, the dollar is actually a privately owned entity marketed and supported by the government.

In 1913, the Federal Reserve System was created in the United States. The Federal Reserve is a network of twelve regional banks that are responsible for overseeing the nation's monetary policy. One of the Federal Reserve's primary functions is to regulate the money supply by controlling the amount of currency in circulation.

Contrary to popular belief, the Federal Reserve is not a government agency. Instead, it is a private corporation that is owned by a group of member banks. These banks hold shares in the Federal Reserve and appoint its board of directors. However, the Federal Reserve's actions are subject to oversight by the government, and its policies are guided by the Federal Reserve Act, which was passed by Congress.

So, what does this mean for our money? Essentially, it means that the government does not own our money, and it does not have complete control over it. The money we use every day is a product of a complex system that involves private banks, the Federal Reserve, and the government.

When the government needs to spend money, it does not simply print more. Instead, it borrows money from the Federal Reserve or sells Treasury bonds to investors. This process adds money to the economy, increasing the money supply. Conversely, when the government wants to reduce the money supply, it can sell Treasury bonds or increase the interest rate charged by the Federal Reserve to member banks.

While the Federal Reserve and private banks play a significant role in the creation and regulation of our money, the government does have some influence. For example, the government can regulate the banking industry, and it can enact policies that encourage or discourage spending.

In conclusion, while the government plays an important role in the regulation of our money, it does not own it. The dollar is a privately owned entity marketed and supported by the government. Understanding this complex relationship is essential to understanding how our monetary system works and how it can be influenced by various actors.

Chapter 4: The Birth of the IRS and its Connection to the Federal Reserve

In 1913, the same year that the Federal Reserve System was created, the Internal Revenue Service (IRS) was also established. The IRS is responsible for collecting taxes and enforcing the tax laws in the United States. While the IRS and the Federal Reserve may seem like two completely unrelated entities, they are, in fact, closely intertwined.

The connection between the Federal Reserve and the IRS lies in the fact that both were established in response to a need for increased government control over the economy. Prior to the establishment of the Federal Reserve, the United States experienced frequent financial crises, and there was a growing sense that the government needed to do more to regulate the economy.

Similarly, the establishment of the IRS was a response to the need for increased government revenue. The United States was growing rapidly, and the government needed more money to fund its operations. The income tax, which was established in 1913, provided a new source of revenue for the government, allowing it to expand its programs and services.

The IRS and the Federal Reserve work closely together to regulate the economy. The Federal Reserve has the power to control the money supply, while the IRS has the power to regulate the flow of money by collecting taxes. By working together, these two entities can influence the economy in significant ways.

In addition to the IRS and the Federal Reserve, Wall Street also plays a crucial role in the economy. Wall Street is the financial center of the United States, and it is where many of the country's largest corporations and financial institutions are located. The government works closely with Wall Street to regulate the economy and ensure its stability.

The relationship between the government, the Federal Reserve, the IRS, and Wall Street is complex, and it is constantly evolving. While each of these entities has its own unique role to play in the economy, they are all working together to achieve a common goal: to ensure the stability and growth of the economy.

In conclusion, the establishment of the IRS in 1913 was a response to the need for increased government revenue, just as the Federal Reserve was established to provide greater government control over the economy. Together with Wall Street, these entities work closely together to regulate the economy and ensure its stability. Understanding the complex relationship between these entities is essential to understanding how the economy works and how it can be influenced by various actors.

Chapter 5: The Silver Standard of 1933 and the Loss of Real Value in Money

In 1933, the United States government abandoned the gold standard and replaced it with the silver standard. Under the silver standard, the government no longer guaranteed that paper money could be exchanged for a fixed amount of gold. Instead, it guaranteed that paper money could be exchanged for a fixed amount of silver.

The abandonment of the gold standard and the adoption of the silver standard marked a significant shift in the value of money. Prior to 1933, the value of money was tied directly to the amount of gold that it could be exchanged for. This meant that the value of money was directly tied to the real world value of gold. However, with the silver standard, the government effectively took the real value out of money.

This move was not without its critics. Many argued that the government's decision to abandon the gold standard was a mistake that would lead to inflation and economic instability. Indeed, the value of the dollar began to decline rapidly following the adoption of the silver standard. By the end of the 1930s, the dollar had lost a significant amount of its value, and the economy was in shambles.

Despite the criticism, the government continued to support the silver standard until 1971, when it was finally abandoned in favor of a fiat currency system. Under the fiat currency system, the government no longer guarantees that paper money can be exchanged for a fixed amount of any commodity. Instead, the value of money is determined by a complex system of supply and demand.

The adoption of the fiat currency system has had significant consequences for the value of money. Since the value of money is no longer tied to any tangible commodity, it has lost all real world value. Today, the value of money is determined by the perception of its worth in the global marketplace, and its value can fluctuate wildly from day to day.

Incredibly, most people are unaware of the history and inner workings of our monetary system. It is not taught in schools, and it is rarely discussed in the media or by politicians. This lack of education has left many people uninformed about the complexities of the monetary system and how it affects their daily lives.

In school, we learn about ancient civilizations such as Egypt, Rome, and Greece, but we are never taught about the history of our own monetary system. It is as if this crucial aspect of our society has been deliberately ignored by those who design our curriculum. It is not surprising that most people are unaware of the intricacies of our monetary system and how it has evolved over the years.

This lack of education has allowed those in power to manipulate and control our monetary system without fear of public scrutiny. The Federal Reserve, the IRS, and Wall Street have been able to operate in secrecy, using their power to benefit the elite at the expense of the average citizen. The lack of education has also allowed politicians to use their power to support these entities, without fear of backlash from

CHAPTER 5: THE SILVER STANDARD OF 1933 AND THE LOSS OF REAL...

the public.

It is time for people to become educated about the monetary system and demand transparency from those in power. We need to understand the history of our monetary system and how it has been used to benefit the few at the expense of the many. By doing so, we can begin to demand real change and create a monetary system that serves the needs of all people, not just the wealthy and powerful.

In conclusion, the lack of education about our monetary system has left many people uninformed about its history and inner workings. It is time for us to demand transparency and to become educated about the system that affects our daily lives. We must demand change and create a system that serves the needs of all people, not just a select few.

Chapter 6: The Introduction of Paper Money

Money is a fascinating concept, and throughout history, it has taken many different forms. From gold and silver coins to paper money, money has evolved to meet the needs of society. However, one thing that remains constant is that all money is essentially a debt note.

When paper money was first introduced, it was essentially a receipt for a deposit of gold or silver. People would store their precious metals at a safe house and receive a paper note that represented the value of their deposit. Eventually, people began trading these notes instead of the actual metal, and paper money was born.

Today, our money is still essentially a debt note. When the Federal Reserve prints money, it is essentially creating debt. This debt is owed to the Federal Reserve, which is owned by the big banks. The banks then loan this money out to people and businesses, creating more debt in the process.

This system of debt creation has its roots in the gold standard, which was abandoned in 1933. Under the gold standard, money was backed by gold, meaning that every dollar had a corresponding amount of gold

CHAPTER 6: THE INTRODUCTION OF PAPER MONEY

held in reserve. However, in 1933, President Franklin D. Roosevelt issued Executive Order 6102, which prohibited the private ownership of gold and required all gold to be turned in to the Federal Reserve. This effectively ended the gold standard and paved the way for the current system of fiat money.

Today, our money has no intrinsic value. It is not backed by gold or any other precious metal. Instead, its value is based on the faith and credit of the United States government. This means that our money is essentially a debt note, backed by the promise of the government to pay it back.

In conclusion, all money is essentially a debt note. Whether it is backed by gold or not, money represents a debt owed by someone to someone else. This debt-based monetary system has its roots in the gold standard and has evolved over time to meet the needs of society. However, it is important to remember that our money is not an objective measure of value, but rather a symbol of the debt we owe to each other.

Chapter 7: Systematic Loopholes

Debt and taxes are two of the most powerful tools in the financial world. When used correctly, they can help you find systematic loopholes that can benefit you financially. Many wealthy individuals have been able to use these tools to keep their entire lives in debt while still profiting and living a carefree, wealthy lifestyle.

One of the key benefits of debt is that it is untaxable. If you know how to handle it correctly, you can keep your entire life in debt and still profit from it. For example, if you buy gold or silver, you have effectively moved the form of your money. You can then use that gold or silver as collateral to take out a loan, which you can then use to buy a cash-flowing asset. By doing this, you are using debt to gain zero dollars in money out, effectively living off your debt.

Of course, not everyone can handle this type of lifestyle. It requires a lot of financial knowledge and discipline to pull off. However, the principle remains the same. By using debt and tax codes to your advantage, you can find systematic loopholes that can benefit you financially.

For example, instead of buying a liability, such as a car or a house that will depreciate in value over time, you could take out a loan to buy a

CHAPTER 7: SYSTEMATIC LOOPHOLES

cash-flowing asset, such as a rental property. This way, you can use the rental income to pay off the loan, effectively using debt to acquire an asset that will provide you with a steady stream of income for years to come.

In conclusion, debt and tax codes are powerful tools that can be used to find systematic loopholes in the financial world. By using debt to acquire cash-flowing assets, you can live off your debt and create a steady stream of income that will provide for you for years to come. However, it is important to remember that this lifestyle is not for everyone, and it requires a lot of financial knowledge and discipline to pull off successfully.

Chapter 8: Recap & Wrap up

After reading this book, it is clear that money is not just a simple medium of exchange. It is a complex system that is controlled by a small group of individuals, with the federal reserve at the top, big banks, businesses, and the government in the middle, and the people at the bottom. It is a pyramid scheme, where the top controls the bottom, and the bottom has little say in how the system is run.

We learned that our money is not backed by anything of tangible value anymore, and has lost all real-world value. We learned that the IRS and the Federal Reserve were both established in 1913 and work together with the government and big businesses to maintain control over the financial system. We also learned that debt and tax codes can be used as tools to find systematic loopholes and benefit financially.

It may seem overwhelming and even discouraging to learn about the true nature of money and the financial system. However, it is important to understand that this is simply the way of money and the world of finances. In order to thrive in this system, we must learn all we can about it and use that knowledge to our advantage.

We must understand the power of debt and tax codes and learn how to use them to our advantage. We must also be aware of the systematic loopholes that exist within the financial system and take advantage of them. However, we must do so with caution and discipline, as it is easy to fall into the trap of debt and lose control of our financial future.

In conclusion, the world of finance can be a daunting and complex system to navigate. But by arming ourselves with knowledge and using it to our advantage, we can thrive in this system and achieve financial success. It is up to us to take control of our financial future and create a life of abundance and prosperity.

SIDE NOTE-Goes Along With Chapter 4

It is a theory that has been circulating for years - the idea that the sinking of the Titanic was not an accident, but rather a well-planned hit job. The Titanic was the largest and most luxurious ship of its time, designed to cater to the wealthiest and most influential people in the world. Yet, on that fateful night in 1912, the ship hit an iceberg and sank, resulting in the deaths of over 1,500 people.

One of the most intriguing aspects of this theory is the involvement of the powerful Rockefeller family and the infamous J.P. Morgan, who conveniently canceled their trip at the last minute, leaving behind their invitations. The most well-known victim of the disaster was John Jacob Astor, one of the wealthiest men in America at the time, with 40% of all of the country's mortgages under his control.

It is believed that Astor, along with many other wealthy and influential individuals on board, were targeted in a hit job to thin out the ranks of the rich and powerful, leaving only the final families in control. The sinking of the Titanic would have been the perfect opportunity to eliminate those who stood in the way of the ultimate goal of consolidating power in the hands of a select few.

While there is no concrete evidence to support this theory, it remains

SIDE NOTE-GOES ALONG WITH CHAPTER 4

a fascinating and intriguing part of the Titanic's legacy. The idea that the sinking of the ship was not an accident, but rather a carefully orchestrated hit job, adds a layer of mystery and intrigue to one of the most tragic events in modern history.

Indeed, it is interesting to note that the sinking of the Titanic occurred in 1912, just a year before the establishment of the Federal Reserve and the IRS in the United States. These institutions have played a major role in shaping the country's financial and economic systems, and their creation marked a significant shift in the way money was managed and controlled in the United States.

Some conspiracy theorists believe that the sinking of the Titanic was somehow connected to the establishment of these institutions, suggesting that there may have been some kind of hidden agenda or ulterior motive behind the disaster. While there is no concrete evidence to support these claims, they do add another layer of intrigue to an already mysterious event.

www.ingramcontent.com/pod-product-compliance
Lightning Source LLC
Chambersburg PA
CBHW070759220526
45467CB00014B/825